MACHINES ON THE FARM

MACHINES

illustrated with photographs

ON THE FARM

Hope Irvin Marston

Dodd, Mead & Company

New York

The photographs in this book are used by permission and through the courtesy of: Allis-Chalmers, 30, 31, 50-51, 52 (bottom), 54, 55, 58, 59; Amco Products (Dynamics Corporation of America), 19; ARPS Division of Chromalloy Farm & Industrial Equipment Co., 63; J. I. Case, 10; Century Engineering Division, Ex-Cell-O Corporation, 29; Deere & Company, 15, 20, 21, 24, 25, 37, 38, 42, 43, 44, 46, 61; Glencoe (Dynamics Corporation of America), 33; Ford Tractor Operations, 6, 8, 9, 13; Gehl Company, 36, 39, 47; International Harvester, 11, 14, 17, 23, 60; John R. Kovar Mfg. Co., 26, 27; L. L. Larson Machine, Inc., 28; Hope Irvin Marston, 56, 57; Massey Ferguson, 34, 45, 52 (top), 53; Sperry-New Holland, 41, 49.

1 2 3 4 5 6 7 8 9 10

Library of Congress Cataloging in Publication Data

Marston, Hope Irvin.
  Machines on the farm.

  Includes index.
  Summary: Explains how farmers use tractors, plows, planters, sprayers, cultivators, balers, combines, and other machines in the production of various crops.
    1. Agricultural machinery—Juvenile literature.
  [1. Agricultural machinery. 2. Machinery. 3. Farms]
  I. Title.
  S675.25.M37   631.3   82-5106
  ISBN 0-396-08070-7   AACR2

This book is dedicated to the three farmers
I know best: my dad, Leslie, and Damaris

Farmers in the United States grow much of the world's food. There are farms throughout the country. Some are very large farms with thousands of acres of land. Some are small farms with fewer than a hundred acres. But to produce good crops on any farm, efficient machines are needed.

A tractor is the farmer's most important piece of machinery. There are different kinds of tractors. This Ford FW-60 is one of the biggest and most modern.

The farmer chooses the size of tractor that has the right amount of power to do his work. The giant FW-60 has four-wheel drive and a 335-horsepower diesel engine. It has 20 forward speeds. Its tilt-up hood makes it easy to service.

The cab on this up-to-date tractor protects the operator from the weather. It has an air conditioner, heater, defroster, AM/FM radio, and tape player.

Few days go by when the farmer does not hitch his tractor to some other piece of equipment to get his work done. This Case Model 1690 is a medium-sized tractor. It has a 90-horsepower diesel engine and 12 forward speeds.

Smaller two-wheel drive tractors are used on many farms. These models often do not have closed-in cabs. But they are powerful enough to do much of the daily work on the farm.

Before seeds are planted, the land has to be plowed. Plowing turns over the soil and covers weeds, dried grass, or cornstalks left over from last year's crop.

A moldboard plow is the most common kind. The moldboard is a curved piece of metal with a strong cutting blade at the bottom called a plowshare. A sharp disk—the coulter wheel—slashes through the weeds and soil in front of each plowshare. The plowshare cuts deep into the soil, and the moldboard turns the soil over.

Plowing a field is tough work. A strong metal bar called the landside, keeps the plowshare running straight. The plowshare, moldboard, and landside together are called a bottom. Plows usually have at least four bottoms. They may have as many as 16. The plow on the opposite page has 12 bottoms.

The chisel plow is another kind. It can dig eight inches into the soil. Its "teeth" vibrate to break up the clumps of soil, tear out the weeds, and mix the leftover "trash" into the ground.

Some farmers use a roll-over plow. This is a moldboard plow with two rows of bottoms mounted in opposite directions. When the farmer gets to the end of his row, he "rolls" the plow over and uses the other row of bottoms as he heads back along the furrow he has just plowed. (A furrow is the shallow trench made behind each bottom of a plow.)

A plowed field is rough and uneven. The large clumps of earth need to be broken up and smoothed out. This is done with a harrow, pulled by a tractor. The metal disks mounted on a bar are called a gang.

Midwestern wheat farmers use huge double-disk harrows with two gangs. This one covers 39 feet in one trip across the field.

The crops a farmer grows can be corn, wheat, oats, barley, cotton, soybeans, hay. No matter what the crop is, it must be planted properly or the harvest will be poor.

A machine called a planter is used for large seeds such as corn. The planter makes a V-shaped trench and drops the seed corn into it at regular intervals. Then it gently covers the kernels by moving the earth in from the sides.

Some planters are adjustable. The rows can be spaced from 30 to 40 inches apart. By adding the right attachment, the farmer can apply fertilizer as he plants.

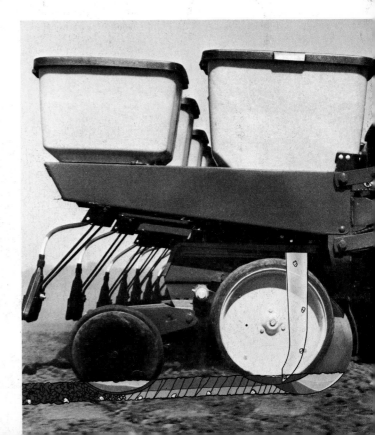

Very small seeds, like those of wheat, are planted with a drill. A storage box called a hopper holds the seeds, and the drill allows them to drop out at an even rate. Grain drills can penetrate dry, firm soil. They place the seeds deep enough to find moisture so they will start to grow.

By using two drills at once, a farmer doubles the amount of seeds planted at one time, and saves time and fuel.

Fertilizer is "food" that plants need if they are going to grow well. This 12-row planter has six tanks for liquid fertilizer. It is folded up while being pulled to the field. When in use it will be opened out.

Weeds rob the soil of nutrients which growing plants need. The farmer can control weeds with chemicals. Sometimes fertilizer and chemicals are applied when the ground is being prepared for planting.

A harrowing machine known as a "Clod-Father" applies chemicals and works them into the soil with its 11-inch teeth that move in a circular motion. Harrowing the chemicals into the soil is more effective than applying them on top and waiting for the rain to work them into the ground.

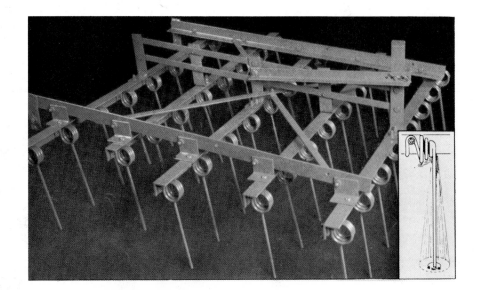

Dry fertilizer can be spread on a field with a broadcaster. This is a spinner-type spreader which forces the fertilizer out in a fine, dry spray. Large broadcasters carry as much as eight tons of fertilizer at one time.

Sprayers are sometimes used to apply liquid fertilizers. They can also spray chemicals to control weeds or insects. Pipelines called booms extend on either side of the machine to spray many rows at a time. This Century sprayer has a 60-foot boom. Farmers sometimes rent machines like sprayers or broadcasters, since they do not need them year round.

Spraying is not the only way to control weeds. Once the plants have started to grow, the field should be cultivated—that is, hoed. A field cultivator has tines that break up crusted soil and dig out weeds. This Allis-Chalmers cultivator has curved tines that vibrate and shatter the soil, destroying even the smallest weeds.

Cultivators can also be used to prepare the ground before planting, to loosen up pasture areas, and to mix dry fertilizers into the soil.

This Glencoe cultivator can cultivate 52 feet of land at one time. It folds up when it is being moved from one place to another.

Hay is grass, such as clover, alfalfa, or timothy, that is grown to feed livestock. Forage, or fodder, is coarsely chopped stalks and leaves of crops that are mixed with hay for feed. Forage is the major part of an animal's diet.

Mowers, rakes, windrowers, conditioners, balers, and choppers are machines used to harvest hay and forage. Some farmers cut their hay with a mower. Then they rake it into long rows called windrows to dry. But most farmers combine mowing and raking by using a mower-conditioner.

A mower-conditioner makes thousands of cuts per minute and slices through a wide path. These machines cut the hay, crush and crimp it to speed drying, and leave it in windrows. If it rains on the windrows, the farmer will "kick them over" with a rake to aid drying.

A baler picks up the hay from the windrow and compresses it into a rectangle called a bale. It ties the bale firmly and forces it out through a chute. A large baler can handle up to 19 tons of hay per hour.

Bales are dropped on the ground or "kicked" onto a wagon pulled behind the baler. A "kicker" saves work, since no one has to come along and pick up the bales.

Some livestock farmers prefer large, round bales of hay. They are made by a different kind of baler. Round bales may be five or six feet in diameter and weigh up to 1,500 pounds.

Round bales of hay can be left in the field until needed, stored in a barn, or put into a feed lot where the cattle eat from them. The big round bales are moved with a bale handler.

Stack wagons are a modern way to handle hay for winter feeding. The hay is picked up from the windrows and compressed under high pressure into huge weather-resistant stacks. These stacks can be left in the field until needed. Stacks weigh from one and a half to six tons. A stack shredder/feeder hitched to a tractor shreds and distributes the hay along the ground in a feed lot or into feed bunks.

Not all hay is baled. "Haylage" is chopped hay or forage that is put into a silo for storage. The crop is cut, chopped, and blown into a self-unloading forage wagon. Then it is hauled to the silo.

Corn is often grown as forage. A corn "head" is attached to a forage chopper. It chops the plants—ears, leaves, and stems—and blows them into the forage wagon.

The loaded forage wagon is taken to the silo. There the forage is unloaded into a blower which whisks it to the top of the silo through a large pipe.

When a farmer's crops are ripe, they have to be harvested. For grain crops a combine is used. A combine is one of the largest farm machines. It does a combination of operations. It cuts the grain and threshes it—removes the grain from the stalks—and cleans it. Some combines are large enough to cut a 35-foot width of grain in one trip across the field.

You can trace the path of the grain through this cutaway of a giant Allis-Chalmers combine.

The grain tank on a big combine can hold as many as 300 bushels. When it is full, the grain is emptied into a wagon or truck and taken to storage, or to market.

Grain must be harvested when it is ripe. To delay is to risk losing the crop. It can get too ripe and fall to the ground. Or wind, rain, or hail could knock the kernels off the stalks. A farmer with hundreds of acres to gather uses several combines in the same field.

A combine is used to harvest soybeans in Iowa . . .

. . . and to harvest rice in Arkansas.

Many acres of corn are picked and husked by using a corn picker. It snaps the ears from the stalks and husks them. The ears can be stored in corn "cribs" until needed for feed.

Other corn is picked and shelled by a combine with a corn head attachment. The ears are snapped from the stalks, then husked and shelled. When the combine's bin is full, the shelled corn is emptied into a truck or wagon.

Cotton is picked by a cotton harvester. The cotton bolls
are blown into a huge basket behind the driver. When the
basket gets full, the cotton is unloaded into a trailer.

Livestock farmers must get rid of the animal waste called manure. Since it makes good fertilizer, farmers pick it up regularly and spread it on fields. The farmer uses a loader mounted on the front of a tractor. The manure is dumped into a spreader and hauled to the field.

The spreader unloads itself as the farmer pulls it along with his tractor.

There are many other machines that farmers use. In northern states farmers must have snow removal machines to clear driveways, barnyards, and feed lots. The equipment may be a scoop or blade mounted on the front of the tractor. Or it might be a giant snowblower attached at the rear.

Perhaps you will be one of the farmers of the future. If so, you will be using machines like the ones you have seen here. Or maybe bigger and better ones.

Index